THIS GUEST BOOK BELONGS TO

_____

BE OUR GUEST

NAME _____

DATE OF VISIT _____

WHERE TRAVELED FROM _____

_____

MESSAGE TO THE HOST

_____

_____

_____

_____

_____

_____

_____

_____

_____

_____

TIPS FOR FUTURE GUESTS

_____

_____

_____

_____

BE OUR GUEST

NAME _____

DATE OF VISIT_____

WHERE TRAVELED FROM _____

_____

MESSAGE TO THE HOST

_____

_____

_____

_____

_____

_____

_____

_____

_____

_____

_____

TIPS FOR FUTURE GUESTS

_____

_____

_____

_____

BE OUR GUEST

NAME _____

DATE OF VISIT _____

WHERE TRAVELED FROM _____

_____

MESSAGE TO THE HOST

_____
_____
_____
_____
_____
_____
_____
_____
_____
_____

TIPS FOR FUTURE GUESTS

_____
_____
_____
_____

BE OUR GUEST

NAME _____

DATE OF VISIT _____

WHERE TRAVELED FROM _____

_____

MESSAGE TO THE HOST

_____
_____
_____
_____
_____
_____
_____
_____
_____
_____
_____

TIPS FOR FUTURE GUESTS

_____
_____
_____
_____

BE OUR GUEST

NAME _____

DATE OF VISIT _____

WHERE TRAVELED FROM _____

_____

MESSAGE TO THE HOST

_____
_____
_____
_____
_____
_____
_____
_____
_____
_____
_____

TIPS FOR FUTURE GUESTS

_____
_____
_____
_____

BE OUR GUEST

NAME _____

DATE OF VISIT _____

WHERE TRAVELED FROM _____

_____

MESSAGE TO THE HOST

_____
_____
_____
_____
_____
_____
_____
_____
_____
_____
_____

TIPS FOR FUTURE GUESTS

_____
_____
_____
_____

BE OUR GUEST

NAME _____

DATE OF VISIT_____

WHERE TRAVELED FROM _____

_____

MESSAGE TO THE HOST

_____

_____

_____

_____

_____

_____

_____

_____

_____

_____

_____

TIPS FOR FUTURE GUESTS

_____

_____

_____

_____

BE OUR GUEST

NAME _____

DATE OF VISIT _____

WHERE TRAVELED FROM _____

_____

MESSAGE TO THE HOST

_____

_____

_____

_____

_____

_____

_____

_____

_____

_____

_____

TIPS FOR FUTURE GUESTS

_____

_____

_____

_____

BE OUR GUEST

NAME _____

DATE OF VISIT _____

WHERE TRAVELED FROM _____

_____

MESSAGE TO THE HOST

_____
_____
_____
_____
_____
_____
_____
_____
_____
_____
_____

TIPS FOR FUTURE GUESTS

_____
_____
_____
_____

BE OUR GUEST

NAME _____

DATE OF VISIT _____

WHERE TRAVELED FROM _____

_____

MESSAGE TO THE HOST

_____

_____

_____

_____

_____

_____

_____

_____

_____

_____

TIPS FOR FUTURE GUESTS

_____

_____

_____

_____

BE OUR GUEST

NAME _____

DATE OF VISIT_____

WHERE TRAVELED FROM _____

_____

MESSAGE TO THE HOST

_____
_____
_____
_____
_____
_____
_____
_____
_____
_____

TIPS FOR FUTURE GUESTS

_____
_____
_____
_____

BE OUR GUEST

NAME _____

DATE OF VISIT _____

WHERE TRAVELED FROM _____

_____

MESSAGE TO THE HOST

_____

_____

_____

_____

_____

_____

_____

_____

_____

_____

_____

TIPS FOR FUTURE GUESTS

_____

_____

_____

_____

BE OUR GUEST

NAME _____

DATE OF VISIT _____

WHERE TRAVELED FROM _____

_____

MESSAGE TO THE HOST

_____
_____
_____
_____
_____
_____
_____
_____
_____
_____
_____

TIPS FOR FUTURE GUESTS

_____
_____
_____
_____

BE OUR GUEST

NAME _____

DATE OF VISIT _____

WHERE TRAVELED FROM _____

_____

MESSAGE TO THE HOST

_____
_____
_____
_____
_____
_____
_____
_____
_____
_____
_____

TIPS FOR FUTURE GUESTS

_____
_____
_____
_____

BE OUR GUEST

NAME _____

DATE OF VISIT _____

WHERE TRAVELED FROM _____

_____

MESSAGE TO THE HOST

_____
_____
_____
_____
_____
_____
_____
_____
_____
_____

TIPS FOR FUTURE GUESTS

_____
_____
_____
_____

BE OUR GUEST

NAME _____

DATE OF VISIT _____

WHERE TRAVELED FROM _____

_____

MESSAGE TO THE HOST

_____
_____
_____
_____
_____
_____
_____
_____
_____
_____
_____

TIPS FOR FUTURE GUESTS

_____
_____
_____
_____

BE OUR GUEST

NAME _____

DATE OF VISIT_____

WHERE TRAVELED FROM _____

_____

MESSAGE TO THE HOST

_____
_____
_____
_____
_____
_____
_____
_____
_____
_____
_____

TIPS FOR FUTURE GUESTS

_____
_____
_____
_____

BE OUR GUEST

NAME _____

DATE OF VISIT _____

WHERE TRAVELED FROM _____

_____

MESSAGE TO THE HOST

_____

_____

_____

_____

_____

_____

_____

_____

_____

_____

_____

TIPS FOR FUTURE GUESTS

_____

_____

_____

_____

BE OUR GUEST

NAME _____

DATE OF VISIT_____

WHERE TRAVELED FROM _____

_____

MESSAGE TO THE HOST

_____
_____
_____
_____
_____
_____
_____
_____
_____
_____
_____

TIPS FOR FUTURE GUESTS

_____
_____
_____
_____

BE OUR GUEST

NAME _____

DATE OF VISIT _____

WHERE TRAVELED FROM _____

_____

MESSAGE TO THE HOST

_____
_____
_____
_____
_____
_____
_____
_____
_____
_____
_____

TIPS FOR FUTURE GUESTS

_____
_____
_____
_____

BE OUR GUEST

NAME _____

DATE OF VISIT _____

WHERE TRAVELED FROM _____

_____

MESSAGE TO THE HOST

_____
_____
_____
_____
_____
_____
_____
_____
_____
_____

TIPS FOR FUTURE GUESTS

_____
_____
_____
_____

BE OUR GUEST

NAME _____

DATE OF VISIT _____

WHERE TRAVELED FROM _____

_____

MESSAGE TO THE HOST

_____
_____
_____
_____
_____
_____
_____
_____
_____
_____
_____
_____

TIPS FOR FUTURE GUESTS

_____
_____
_____
_____

BE OUR GUEST

NAME _____

DATE OF VISIT _____

WHERE TRAVELED FROM _____

_____

MESSAGE TO THE HOST

_____

_____

_____

_____

_____

_____

_____

_____

_____

_____

TIPS FOR FUTURE GUESTS

_____

_____

_____

_____

BE OUR GUEST

NAME _____

DATE OF VISIT_____

WHERE TRAVELED FROM _____

_____

MESSAGE TO THE HOST

_____

_____

_____

_____

_____

_____

_____

_____

_____

_____

_____

TIPS FOR FUTURE GUESTS

_____

_____

_____

_____

BE OUR GUEST

NAME _____

DATE OF VISIT_____

WHERE TRAVELED FROM _____

_____

MESSAGE TO THE HOST

_____

_____

_____

_____

_____

_____

_____

_____

_____

_____

TIPS FOR FUTURE GUESTS

_____

_____

_____

_____

BE OUR GUEST

NAME _____

DATE OF VISIT_____

WHERE TRAVELED FROM _____

_____

MESSAGE TO THE HOST

_____
_____
_____
_____
_____
_____
_____
_____
_____
_____

TIPS FOR FUTURE GUESTS

_____
_____
_____
_____

BE OUR GUEST

NAME _____

DATE OF VISIT _____

WHERE TRAVELED FROM _____

_____

MESSAGE TO THE HOST

_____

_____

_____

_____

_____

_____

_____

_____

_____

_____

_____

TIPS FOR FUTURE GUESTS

_____

_____

_____

_____

BE OUR GUEST

NAME _____

DATE OF VISIT _____

WHERE TRAVELED FROM _____

_____

MESSAGE TO THE HOST

_____
_____
_____
_____
_____
_____
_____
_____
_____
_____
_____

TIPS FOR FUTURE GUESTS

_____
_____
_____
_____

BE OUR GUEST

NAME _____

DATE OF VISIT_____

WHERE TRAVELED FROM _____

_____

MESSAGE TO THE HOST

_____
_____
_____
_____
_____
_____
_____
_____
_____
_____
_____

TIPS FOR FUTURE GUESTS

_____
_____
_____
_____

BE OUR GUEST

NAME _____

DATE OF VISIT _____

WHERE TRAVELED FROM _____

_____

MESSAGE TO THE HOST

_____
_____
_____
_____
_____
_____
_____
_____
_____
_____
_____

TIPS FOR FUTURE GUESTS

_____
_____
_____
_____

BE OUR GUEST

NAME _____

DATE OF VISIT _____

WHERE TRAVELED FROM _____

_____

MESSAGE TO THE HOST

_____

_____

_____

_____

_____

_____

_____

_____

_____

_____

TIPS FOR FUTURE GUESTS

_____

_____

_____

_____

BE OUR GUEST

NAME _____

DATE OF VISIT_____

WHERE TRAVELED FROM _____

_____

MESSAGE TO THE HOST

_____

_____

_____

_____

_____

_____

_____

_____

_____

_____

_____

TIPS FOR FUTURE GUESTS

_____

_____

_____

_____

BE OUR GUEST

NAME _____

DATE OF VISIT _____

WHERE TRAVELED FROM _____

_____

MESSAGE TO THE HOST

_____

_____

_____

_____

_____

_____

_____

_____

_____

_____

TIPS FOR FUTURE GUESTS

_____

_____

_____

_____

BE OUR GUEST

NAME _____

DATE OF VISIT_____

WHERE TRAVELED FROM _____

_____

MESSAGE TO THE HOST

_____
_____
_____
_____
_____
_____
_____
_____
_____
_____
_____
_____

TIPS FOR FUTURE GUESTS

_____
_____
_____
_____

BE OUR GUEST

NAME _____

DATE OF VISIT_____

WHERE TRAVELED FROM _____

_____

MESSAGE TO THE HOST

_____
_____
_____
_____
_____
_____
_____
_____
_____
_____
_____

TIPS FOR FUTURE GUESTS

_____
_____
_____
_____

BE OUR GUEST

NAME _____

DATE OF VISIT _____

WHERE TRAVELED FROM _____

_____

MESSAGE TO THE HOST

_____
_____
_____
_____
_____
_____
_____
_____
_____
_____
_____
_____

TIPS FOR FUTURE GUESTS

_____
_____
_____
_____

BE OUR GUEST

NAME _____

DATE OF VISIT _____

WHERE TRAVELED FROM _____

_____

MESSAGE TO THE HOST

_____
_____
_____
_____
_____
_____
_____
_____
_____
_____
_____

TIPS FOR FUTURE GUESTS

_____
_____
_____
_____

BE OUR GUEST

NAME _____

DATE OF VISIT_____

WHERE TRAVELED FROM _____

_____

MESSAGE TO THE HOST

_____

_____

_____

_____

_____

_____

_____

_____

_____

_____

TIPS FOR FUTURE GUESTS

_____

_____

_____

_____

BE OUR GUEST

NAME _____

DATE OF VISIT _____

WHERE TRAVELED FROM _____

_____

MESSAGE TO THE HOST

_____

_____

_____

_____

_____

_____

_____

_____

_____

_____

TIPS FOR FUTURE GUESTS

_____

_____

_____

_____

BE OUR GUEST

NAME _____

DATE OF VISIT _____

WHERE TRAVELED FROM _____

_____

MESSAGE TO THE HOST

_____
_____
_____
_____
_____
_____
_____
_____
_____
_____
_____
_____
_____

TIPS FOR FUTURE GUESTS

_____
_____
_____
_____

BE OUR GUEST

NAME _____

DATE OF VISIT_____

WHERE TRAVELED FROM _____

_____

MESSAGE TO THE HOST

_____
_____
_____
_____
_____
_____
_____
_____
_____
_____
_____

TIPS FOR FUTURE GUESTS

_____
_____
_____
_____

BE OUR GUEST

NAME _____

DATE OF VISIT _____

WHERE TRAVELED FROM _____

_____

MESSAGE TO THE HOST

_____
_____
_____
_____
_____
_____
_____
_____
_____
_____
_____
_____

TIPS FOR FUTURE GUESTS

_____
_____
_____
_____

BE OUR GUEST

NAME _____

DATE OF VISIT _____

WHERE TRAVELED FROM _____

_____

MESSAGE TO THE HOST

_____

_____

_____

_____

_____

_____

_____

_____

_____

_____

_____

TIPS FOR FUTURE GUESTS

_____

_____

_____

_____

BE OUR GUEST

NAME _____

DATE OF VISIT _____

WHERE TRAVELED FROM _____

_____

MESSAGE TO THE HOST

_____

_____

_____

_____

_____

_____

_____

_____

_____

_____

_____

TIPS FOR FUTURE GUESTS

_____

_____

_____

_____

BE OUR GUEST

NAME _____

DATE OF VISIT _____

WHERE TRAVELED FROM _____

_____

MESSAGE TO THE HOST

_____

_____

_____

_____

_____

_____

_____

_____

_____

_____

_____

TIPS FOR FUTURE GUESTS

_____

_____

_____

_____

BE OUR GUEST

NAME _____

DATE OF VISIT _____

WHERE TRAVELED FROM _____

_____

MESSAGE TO THE HOST

_____
_____
_____
_____
_____
_____
_____
_____
_____
_____
_____

TIPS FOR FUTURE GUESTS

_____
_____
_____
_____

BE OUR GUEST

NAME _____

DATE OF VISIT_____

WHERE TRAVELED FROM _____

_____

MESSAGE TO THE HOST

_____
_____
_____
_____
_____
_____
_____
_____
_____
_____
_____

TIPS FOR FUTURE GUESTS

_____
_____
_____
_____

BE OUR GUEST

NAME _____

DATE OF VISIT_____

WHERE TRAVELED FROM _____

_____

MESSAGE TO THE HOST

_____

_____

_____

_____

_____

_____

_____

_____

_____

_____

_____

TIPS FOR FUTURE GUESTS

_____

_____

_____

_____

BE OUR GUEST

NAME _____

DATE OF VISIT _____

WHERE TRAVELED FROM _____

_____

MESSAGE TO THE HOST

_____
_____
_____
_____
_____
_____
_____
_____
_____
_____

TIPS FOR FUTURE GUESTS

_____
_____
_____
_____

BE OUR GUEST

NAME _____

DATE OF VISIT_____

WHERE TRAVELED FROM _____

_____

MESSAGE TO THE HOST

_____
_____
_____
_____
_____
_____
_____
_____
_____
_____
_____

TIPS FOR FUTURE GUESTS

_____
_____
_____
_____

BE OUR GUEST

NAME _____

DATE OF VISIT _____

WHERE TRAVELED FROM _____

_____

MESSAGE TO THE HOST

_____

_____

_____

_____

_____

_____

_____

_____

_____

_____

_____

TIPS FOR FUTURE GUESTS

_____

_____

_____

_____

BE OUR GUEST

NAME _____

DATE OF VISIT _____

WHERE TRAVELED FROM _____

_____

MESSAGE TO THE HOST

_____
_____
_____
_____
_____
_____
_____
_____
_____
_____
_____

TIPS FOR FUTURE GUESTS

_____
_____
_____
_____

BE OUR GUEST

NAME _____

DATE OF VISIT_____

WHERE TRAVELED FROM _____

_____

MESSAGE TO THE HOST

_____

_____

_____

_____

_____

_____

_____

_____

_____

_____

TIPS FOR FUTURE GUESTS

_____

_____

_____

_____

BE OUR GUEST

NAME _____

DATE OF VISIT_____

WHERE TRAVELED FROM _____

_____

MESSAGE TO THE HOST

_____
_____
_____
_____
_____
_____
_____
_____
_____
_____
_____

TIPS FOR FUTURE GUESTS

_____
_____
_____
_____

BE OUR GUEST

NAME _____

DATE OF VISIT_____

WHERE TRAVELED FROM _____

_____

MESSAGE TO THE HOST

_____

_____

_____

_____

_____

_____

_____

_____

_____

_____

TIPS FOR FUTURE GUESTS

_____

_____

_____

_____

BE OUR GUEST

NAME _____

DATE OF VISIT_____

WHERE TRAVELED FROM _____

_____

MESSAGE TO THE HOST

_____
_____
_____
_____
_____
_____
_____
_____
_____
_____

TIPS FOR FUTURE GUESTS

_____
_____
_____
_____

BE OUR GUEST

NAME _____

DATE OF VISIT_____

WHERE TRAVELED FROM _____

_____

MESSAGE TO THE HOST

_____

_____

_____

_____

_____

_____

_____

_____

_____

_____

_____

TIPS FOR FUTURE GUESTS

_____

_____

_____

_____

BE OUR GUEST

NAME _____

DATE OF VISIT _____

WHERE TRAVELED FROM _____

_____

MESSAGE TO THE HOST

_____
_____
_____
_____
_____
_____
_____
_____
_____
_____
_____

TIPS FOR FUTURE GUESTS

_____
_____
_____
_____

BE OUR GUEST

NAME _____

DATE OF VISIT_____

WHERE TRAVELED FROM _____

_____

MESSAGE TO THE HOST

_____

_____

_____

_____

_____

_____

_____

_____

_____

_____

TIPS FOR FUTURE GUESTS

_____

_____

_____

_____

BE OUR GUEST

NAME _____

DATE OF VISIT_____

WHERE TRAVELED FROM _____

_____

MESSAGE TO THE HOST

_____
_____
_____
_____
_____
_____
_____
_____
_____
_____
_____

TIPS FOR FUTURE GUESTS

_____
_____
_____
_____

BE OUR GUEST

NAME _____

DATE OF VISIT_____

WHERE TRAVELED FROM _____

_____

MESSAGE TO THE HOST

_____

_____

_____

_____

_____

_____

_____

_____

_____

_____

TIPS FOR FUTURE GUESTS

_____

_____

_____

_____

BE OUR GUEST

NAME _____

DATE OF VISIT _____

WHERE TRAVELED FROM _____

_____

MESSAGE TO THE HOST

_____

_____

_____

_____

_____

_____

_____

_____

_____

_____

TIPS FOR FUTURE GUESTS

_____

_____

_____

_____

BE OUR GUEST

NAME _____

DATE OF VISIT_____

WHERE TRAVELED FROM _____

_____

MESSAGE TO THE HOST

_____
_____
_____
_____
_____
_____
_____
_____
_____
_____
_____

TIPS FOR FUTURE GUESTS

_____
_____
_____
_____

BE OUR GUEST

NAME _____

DATE OF VISIT _____

WHERE TRAVELED FROM _____

_____

MESSAGE TO THE HOST

_____
_____
_____
_____
_____
_____
_____
_____
_____
_____
_____

TIPS FOR FUTURE GUESTS

_____
_____
_____
_____

BE OUR GUEST

NAME _____

DATE OF VISIT _____

WHERE TRAVELED FROM _____

_____

MESSAGE TO THE HOST

_____

_____

_____

_____

_____

_____

_____

_____

_____

_____

TIPS FOR FUTURE GUESTS

_____

_____

_____

_____

BE OUR GUEST

NAME _____

DATE OF VISIT_____

WHERE TRAVELED FROM _____

_____

MESSAGE TO THE HOST

_____

_____

_____

_____

_____

_____

_____

_____

_____

_____

TIPS FOR FUTURE GUESTS

_____

_____

_____

_____

BE OUR GUEST

NAME _____

DATE OF VISIT _____

WHERE TRAVELED FROM _____

_____

MESSAGE TO THE HOST

_____

_____

_____

_____

_____

_____

_____

_____

_____

_____

TIPS FOR FUTURE GUESTS

_____

_____

_____

_____

BE OUR GUEST

NAME _____

DATE OF VISIT_____

WHERE TRAVELED FROM _____

_____

MESSAGE TO THE HOST

_____

_____

_____

_____

_____

_____

_____

_____

_____

_____

TIPS FOR FUTURE GUESTS

_____

_____

_____

_____

BE OUR GUEST

NAME _____

DATE OF VISIT_____

WHERE TRAVELED FROM _____

_____

MESSAGE TO THE HOST

_____

_____

_____

_____

_____

_____

_____

_____

_____

_____

TIPS FOR FUTURE GUESTS

_____

_____

_____

_____

BE OUR GUEST

NAME _____

DATE OF VISIT_____

WHERE TRAVELED FROM _____

_____

MESSAGE TO THE HOST

_____
_____
_____
_____
_____
_____
_____
_____
_____
_____
_____

TIPS FOR FUTURE GUESTS

_____
_____
_____
_____

BE OUR GUEST

NAME _____

DATE OF VISIT_____

WHERE TRAVELED FROM _____

_____

MESSAGE TO THE HOST

_____
_____
_____
_____
_____
_____
_____
_____
_____
_____
_____

TIPS FOR FUTURE GUESTS

_____
_____
_____
_____

BE OUR GUEST

NAME _____

DATE OF VISIT_____

WHERE TRAVELED FROM _____

_____

MESSAGE TO THE HOST

_____
_____
_____
_____
_____
_____
_____
_____
_____
_____
_____

TIPS FOR FUTURE GUESTS

_____
_____
_____
_____

BE OUR GUEST

NAME _____

DATE OF VISIT _____

WHERE TRAVELED FROM _____

_____

MESSAGE TO THE HOST

_____
_____
_____
_____
_____
_____
_____
_____
_____
_____
_____

TIPS FOR FUTURE GUESTS

_____
_____
_____
_____

BE OUR GUEST

NAME _____

DATE OF VISIT _____

WHERE TRAVELED FROM _____

_____

MESSAGE TO THE HOST

_____
_____
_____
_____
_____
_____
_____
_____
_____
_____
_____

TIPS FOR FUTURE GUESTS

_____
_____
_____
_____

BE OUR GUEST

NAME _____

DATE OF VISIT_____

WHERE TRAVELED FROM _____

_____

MESSAGE TO THE HOST

_____

_____

_____

_____

_____

_____

_____

_____

_____

_____

_____

TIPS FOR FUTURE GUESTS

_____

_____

_____

BE OUR GUEST

NAME _____

DATE OF VISIT _____

WHERE TRAVELED FROM _____

_____

MESSAGE TO THE HOST

_____
_____
_____
_____
_____
_____
_____
_____
_____
_____

TIPS FOR FUTURE GUESTS

_____
_____
_____
_____

BE OUR GUEST

NAME _____

DATE OF VISIT _____

WHERE TRAVELED FROM _____

_____

MESSAGE TO THE HOST

_____
_____
_____
_____
_____
_____
_____
_____
_____
_____

TIPS FOR FUTURE GUESTS

_____
_____
_____
_____

BE OUR GUEST

NAME _____

DATE OF VISIT_____

WHERE TRAVELED FROM _____

_____

MESSAGE TO THE HOST

_____
_____
_____
_____
_____
_____
_____
_____
_____
_____
_____

TIPS FOR FUTURE GUESTS

_____
_____
_____
_____

BE OUR GUEST

NAME _____

DATE OF VISIT_____

WHERE TRAVELED FROM _____

_____

MESSAGE TO THE HOST

_____

_____

_____

_____

_____

_____

_____

_____

_____

_____

TIPS FOR FUTURE GUESTS

_____

_____

_____

_____

BE OUR GUEST

NAME _____

DATE OF VISIT _____

WHERE TRAVELED FROM _____

_____

MESSAGE TO THE HOST

_____

_____

_____

_____

_____

_____

_____

_____

_____

_____

_____

TIPS FOR FUTURE GUESTS

_____

_____

_____

_____

BE OUR GUEST

NAME _____

DATE OF VISIT_____

WHERE TRAVELED FROM _____

_____

MESSAGE TO THE HOST

_____

_____

_____

_____

_____

_____

_____

_____

_____

_____

TIPS FOR FUTURE GUESTS

_____

_____

_____

_____

BE OUR GUEST

NAME _____

DATE OF VISIT _____

WHERE TRAVELED FROM _____

_____

MESSAGE TO THE HOST

_____
_____
_____
_____
_____
_____
_____
_____
_____
_____
_____
_____

TIPS FOR FUTURE GUESTS

_____
_____
_____
_____

BE OUR GUEST

NAME _____

DATE OF VISIT_____

WHERE TRAVELED FROM _____

_____

MESSAGE TO THE HOST

_____

_____

_____

_____

_____

_____

_____

_____

_____

_____

_____

TIPS FOR FUTURE GUESTS

_____

_____

_____

_____

BE OUR GUEST

NAME _____

DATE OF VISIT_____

WHERE TRAVELED FROM _____

_____

MESSAGE TO THE HOST

_____
_____
_____
_____
_____
_____
_____
_____
_____
_____
_____

TIPS FOR FUTURE GUESTS

_____
_____
_____
_____

BE OUR GUEST

NAME _____

DATE OF VISIT_____

WHERE TRAVELED FROM _____

_____

MESSAGE TO THE HOST

_____

_____

_____

_____

_____

_____

_____

_____

_____

_____

_____

TIPS FOR FUTURE GUESTS

_____

_____

_____

_____

BE OUR GUEST

NAME _____

DATE OF VISIT _____

WHERE TRAVELED FROM _____

_____

MESSAGE TO THE HOST

_____
_____
_____
_____
_____
_____
_____
_____
_____
_____

TIPS FOR FUTURE GUESTS

_____
_____
_____
_____

BE OUR GUEST

NAME _____

DATE OF VISIT _____

WHERE TRAVELED FROM _____

_____

MESSAGE TO THE HOST

_____

_____

_____

_____

_____

_____

_____

_____

_____

_____

TIPS FOR FUTURE GUESTS

_____

_____

_____

_____

BE OUR GUEST

NAME _____

DATE OF VISIT _____

WHERE TRAVELED FROM _____

_____

MESSAGE TO THE HOST

_____

_____

_____

_____

_____

_____

_____

_____

_____

_____

TIPS FOR FUTURE GUESTS

_____

_____

_____

_____

BE OUR GUEST

NAME _____

DATE OF VISIT _____

WHERE TRAVELED FROM _____

_____

MESSAGE TO THE HOST

_____

_____

_____

_____

_____

_____

_____

_____

_____

_____

TIPS FOR FUTURE GUESTS

_____

_____

_____

_____

BE OUR GUEST

NAME _____

DATE OF VISIT_____

WHERE TRAVELED FROM _____

_____

MESSAGE TO THE HOST

_____
_____
_____
_____
_____
_____
_____
_____
_____
_____
_____

TIPS FOR FUTURE GUESTS

_____
_____
_____
_____

BE OUR GUEST

NAME _____

DATE OF VISIT_____

WHERE TRAVELED FROM _____

_____

MESSAGE TO THE HOST

_____

_____

_____

_____

_____

_____

_____

_____

_____

_____

_____

TIPS FOR FUTURE GUESTS

_____

_____

_____

_____

BE OUR GUEST

NAME _____

DATE OF VISIT _____

WHERE TRAVELED FROM _____

_____

MESSAGE TO THE HOST

_____

_____

_____

_____

_____

_____

_____

_____

_____

_____

TIPS FOR FUTURE GUESTS

_____

_____

_____

_____

BE OUR GUEST

NAME _____

DATE OF VISIT _____

WHERE TRAVELED FROM _____

_____

MESSAGE TO THE HOST

_____

_____

_____

_____

_____

_____

_____

_____

_____

_____

TIPS FOR FUTURE GUESTS

_____

_____

_____

_____

BE OUR GUEST

NAME _____

DATE OF VISIT _____

WHERE TRAVELED FROM _____

_____

MESSAGE TO THE HOST

_____

_____

_____

_____

_____

_____

_____

_____

_____

_____

_____

TIPS FOR FUTURE GUESTS

_____

_____

_____

_____

BE OUR GUEST

NAME _____

DATE OF VISIT_____

WHERE TRAVELED FROM _____

_____

MESSAGE TO THE HOST

_____
_____
_____
_____
_____
_____
_____
_____
_____
_____
_____

TIPS FOR FUTURE GUESTS

_____
_____
_____
_____

BE OUR GUEST

NAME _____

DATE OF VISIT_____

WHERE TRAVELED FROM _____

_____

MESSAGE TO THE HOST

_____

_____

_____

_____

_____

_____

_____

_____

_____

_____

TIPS FOR FUTURE GUESTS

_____

_____

_____

_____

BE OUR GUEST

NAME _____

DATE OF VISIT _____

WHERE TRAVELED FROM _____

_____

MESSAGE TO THE HOST

_____
_____
_____
_____
_____
_____
_____
_____
_____
_____
_____

TIPS FOR FUTURE GUESTS

_____
_____
_____
_____

BE OUR GUEST

NAME _____

DATE OF VISIT_____

WHERE TRAVELED FROM _____

_____

MESSAGE TO THE HOST

_____

_____

_____

_____

_____

_____

_____

_____

_____

_____

TIPS FOR FUTURE GUESTS

_____

_____

_____

_____

BE OUR GUEST

NAME _____

DATE OF VISIT _____

WHERE TRAVELED FROM _____

_____

MESSAGE TO THE HOST

_____
_____
_____
_____
_____
_____
_____
_____
_____
_____
_____

TIPS FOR FUTURE GUESTS

_____
_____
_____
_____

BE OUR GUEST

NAME _____

DATE OF VISIT _____

WHERE TRAVELED FROM _____

_____

MESSAGE TO THE HOST

_____
_____
_____
_____
_____
_____
_____
_____
_____
_____

TIPS FOR FUTURE GUESTS

_____
_____
_____
_____

Printed in Great Britain
by Amazon